E PAR
Parker, Victoria.
Hard or soft / Victoria
Parker.

Is it...?

Hard or Soft

Vic Parker

Raintree

Chicago, Illinois

Color Reproduction by Dot Gradations Ltd, UK.
Printed and bound in China by South China Printing Company.
09 08 07 06 05
10 9 8 7 6 5 4 3 2 1

Library of Congress Cataloging-in-Publication Data:
Parker, Victoria.
  Hard or soft / Victoria Parker.
      p. cm. — (Is it?)
Summary: Shows differences between things that are hard and things that
are soft.
Includes index.
  ISBN 1-4109-0765-1 (lib. bdg.) — ISBN 1-4109-0770-8 (pbk.)
  1. Hardness—Juvenile literature. [1. Hardness.] I. Title. II.
Series: Parker, Victoria. Is it?
  TA418.42.P37 2004
  620.1'126—dc22
                              2003021643

Acknowledgments
The publishers would like to thank Gareth Boden for permission to reproduce photographs.

Cover photograph reproduced with permission of Gareth Boden.

Every effort has been made to contact copyright holders of any material reproduced in this book. Any omissions will be rectified in subsequent printings if notice is given to the publishers.

Some words are shown in bold, **like this**. You can find out what they mean by looking at the glossary on page 24.

Contents

A Treasure Hunt

At school, we are learning about hard and soft things.

We will bring in things from home.

Hunt for Something Hard

Do you see something hard in the dress-up box?

Sunglasses are hard.
I will take these to school.

7

9

Toys

Here are some hard and soft toys.

Which ones will we take to school?

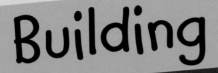

Building

We can build a tall tower with these hard blocks.

12

We can roll logs of soft, squishy clay.

Art

Pencil

Paintbrush

We can make a picture with pencils and paintbrushes.

Is the **tip** of a pencil soft or hard?

Is the tip of a paintbrush soft or hard?

Hard Hats

bicycle helmet

These hats are hard.

horse riding helmet

Can you think of some other kinds of hard hats?

Soft and Clean

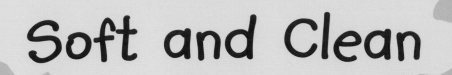

Time to clean up!
A sponge and towel are soft.

I can brush my teeth with soft, squishy toothpaste.

Soft and Sweet

What is inside this hard **mold**?

At School

soft things

Here is our collection of hard and soft things.

hard things

Glossary

mold kind of metal, glass, or plastic dish that has different designs on it. When something soft is poured into a mold, it takes on the shape of the mold.

tip one end of something

Index